TX
652
.W83

Würf, Karl

To serve man

TO SERVE
MAN

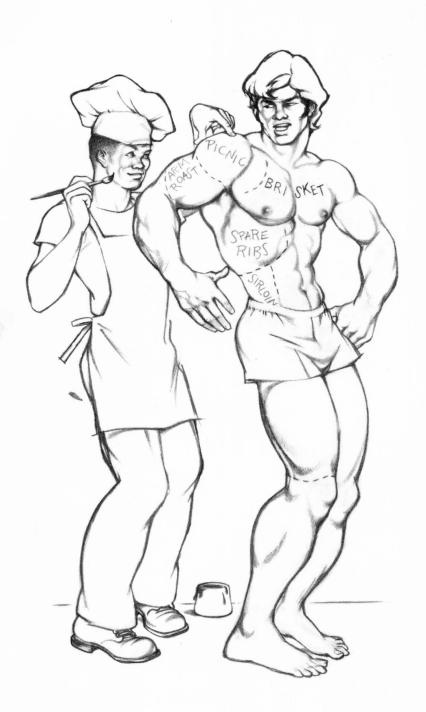

TO SERVE MAN:

a cookbook for people

by Karl Würf
illustrated by Jack Bozzi
foreword by Margaret St. Clair

Owlswick Press
Philadelphia
1976

TX
652
. W83

Published by
the Owlswick Press
Box 8243, Philadelphia PA 19101;
manufactured in the United States of America.

International Standard Book Number 0 913896 05 5
Library of Congress Card Number 76-4348

[iv]

To Damon Knight

for the idea,
the title,
and his kind permission to use both

For their many culinary suggestions for and corrections to this work, the author wishes to thank the Mesdames Dian Crayne, Ann Dietz, Nancy Dills, Ann McKnight, and Mirian Meschkow. Invaluable professional assistance was given by David B. Garmise and Seth Glick, MDs, and by Sidney A. Cochran, Jr., and David J. Williams, III, Esqs., for which the author is also very grateful. Thanks are owed to the Physical Education Department of Miskatonic University, to the College of the Unholy Names' weightlifting team, and to the offensive line of the Arkham *Shamblers* for the raw materials they contributed to this work.

CONTENTS

TO SERVE
MAN

FOREWORD

Incorporation is the ultimate intimacy. The Yankee whaling ship captain who, asked if he knew so-and-so, thundered in reply, "Know that man! Why, I ate that man's uncle!" was expressing the belief that, by incorporating the uncle, he had established a permanent bond with the uncle's whole clan. Any thoughtful person must agree with him. There is no form of carnal knowledge so complete as that of knowing how somebody tastes.

Incorporation is not necessarily accompanied by ill-will. The happy smile on the face of the would-be incorporator (he is the one wearing the chef's hat) in the illustrations to this book is, I believe, psychologically correct. Nietzsche observes that the wolf does not devour lambs because he hates them; he loves lambs. Eros and Thanatos, to paraphrase Freud, meet in the incorporator's throat.

There may be more argument possible about the choice of a person to incorporate. Karl Würf believes that the best donor would be an athlete who has had to diet down to a particular weight class. I think that such a donor would be passable for smoking, pickling, or any sort of long, slow cooking, such as braising or stewing. But for steaks, oven roasts, or chops, a less muscular donor would be preferable. *Pace* Mr. Würf, maximum tenderness and succulence would probably be found in a young, healthy office worker. Fat should be delicately marbled all through the meat, not slathered in a thick layer on the outside.

Once the donor is settled on—potentially a matter of some difficulty—the incorporator has the opportunity to show his creativity by working out something appropriate for special occasions. There is a certain crassness in treating the actual incorporation like any other meal. I can give only a few suggestions here.

The holidays—Christmas and New Year's—are usually celebrated with some sort of office or on-the-job party. Liquor flows plentifully on these occasions, and some sort of hangover next morning is almost inevitable. What could be nicer than to kill two birds with one stone, so to speak, and cope with the hangover with the following dish made from a late drinking companion? For Mexican Tripe:

> 2 pounds Person stomach
> 2 onions
> Garlic, cumin seed, oregano
> 6 dry Mexican chiles
> 2 quarts water
> 1 can garbanzos
> Salt

Wash stomach and cut in strips. Simmer with the onions in the water until strips are almost dissolved. Meantime, put the chiles, 3 or more cloves of garlic, at least a tablespoon of cumin and a generous pinch of oregano in a cup of water and boil until soft. Whirl in a blender until homogeneous. Add with the can of garbanzos to the tripe. Taste for salt. Serve in deep soup plates with hot tortillas. Serves 4. This is a fine hot dish, at first startling and then soothing to an upset stomach. "Un menudo es muy bueno para el crudo."

The appropriate dish for Valentine's Day is too obvious to need mentioning. Gilt cardboard arrows around the covered casserole are a nice touch. And for Washington's birthday the incorporator may like to use a real hatchet, instead of a plastic one, in the table decorations.

Memorial Day is fittingly observed by presenting *Restes d'Homme* (remains hash) in oblong pastry cases.

There is no human dish that is especially appropriate to the Glorious Fourth; but perhaps I should recount, as a warning, the fate of two would-be incorporators who *thought* that there was.

This dim-witted duo were struck by the similarity of sound between "bomb" (as in "the bombs bursting in air") in our national anthem, and the French word *bombe.* Not realizing that the *bombe* is a fancy ice-cream dish frozen in layers, and offers no opportunity for presenting any part of a human, they decided to use their donor in a *bombe.*

In the nervous excitement of preparation, they got the wrong book. Assuming the saltpeter and charcoal to be part of some curing process, they followed the book's instructions to the letter, with the result that they scattered bits of themselves and their donor over half the county. It was a sad waste of good protein, and the only bright spot was that the explosion did eliminate three consumers of the increasingly limited world food supply.

Labor Day is one of the very best times for incorporation. There is an economy, a completeness of utilization, possible then that cannot but appeal to the tidy mind.

It is not only that the large group usually present at a Labor Day barbecue makes good and prompt use of the entire donor—no tiresome leftovers, no jazz about deep freezing or pickling—but there is also a further economy possible that will make it an especial attraction to the organic gardener. In September many vegetable crops are coming into their own—brussels sprouts, broccoli, parsnips, to name a few—and they will all benefit from an application of wood ashes (from the barbecue pit) and bone meal (from the donor). Wood ashes supply potash, bone meal supplies phosphorus, and both contain some nitrogen. Any good cookbook will supply a recipe for barbecue sauce.

Conventional fare for a Halloween party is apple cider and doughnuts. But if you want to serve more of a meal, and surprise your guests with something both unusual and appropriate, nothing is nicer than Offal (variety meat) Soup:

1-1/2 pounds Person stomach
3 onions

2 quarts salted water
3 cups diced Person heart
3 cups diced Person kidney
3 cups diced Person liver
3 small red peppers

Cook the stomach and the onions in the salted water until tender. Then cut the stomach into tiny dice, add the heart, liver, and kidney, and simmer all together until done. Add cut-up red peppers after ten minutes, and increase the water to four quarts. Taste for seasoning, and serve garnished with chopped green onions. Serves 21.

Thanksgiving Day may be observed with Minceman Pie (*which see*) and the crust offers a way to use up some of the lard you tried out from your donor.

We have made the circuit of the year with incorporation, and are back at the office party again. But let nobody think that Tipsy Pudding would be an appropriate presentation of a drunken un-friend he encountered at the office binge. Tipsy Pudding is not made of anybody. It is a rich, sweet dessert that involves a liberal amount of rum.

A final note: despite the exercise of culinary skill (the recipes in this book are excellent), an occasional incorporator may suffer from a certain after-meal malaise—the whips, the butterflies, the jangles—that is partly of the body and partly of the soul. It is the kind of thing that used to be called "existential." It is a miserable way to feel.

There is little help to be looked for in this fix from

Yoga, transcendental meditation, or the family psychiatrist. (After all, the sufferer *did* eat the guy.) The thing for him to do is to concentrate on realizing that the feeling will abate in time. Meanwhile, baking soda helps as much as anything.

Margaret St. Clair

Manchester, California
1 April 1975

INTRODUCTION

Why eat Man? Usually, the harder question to answer is, why not? After all, Man is a large, plentiful (some say *too* plentiful) animal. Unusually choice specimens run about 240 pounds, undressed weight, with a yield of up to 60% edible meat. Man can be prepared for table in many appetizing ways, as detailed elsewhere in this book. And, above all, man is *available*.

Oddly enough, cannibalism *eo nomine* isn't even against the law in most jurisdictions, although it is quite difficult to eat someone without breaking a few of the laws, ordinances, and regulations against premeditated and unpremeditated murder, voluntary and involuntary manslaughter, assault with intent to kill, aggravated assault, assault with intent to maim, kidnapping, peonage, false imprisonment, aggravated arson, piracy *jure gentium,* robbery, larceny, depriving a citizen of his civil rights, unlicensed operation of a hearse, and distribution in commerce of uninspected meat. Nevertheless, the practice can be traced as early as the Lower Pleistocene and probably started back about the time our ancestors first thought about coming down from the trees.

More recently, the custom of eating the sacred king became so well established that there is a word from the Greeks for it: basilophagy. On a less formal basis, long wars have often made cannibalism necessary. For an example, during the Thirty Years War, prowling armies so devastated Europe that there was little for foraging parties to garner but stray soldiers from the other side; and even in modern times, being eaten is one of the hazards of embezzling the troops' pay. And, of course, cannibalism is the traditional last resort of explorers whose enthusiasm outreaches their provisions—on down to the latest example of the practice, for whatever motive, to hit the headlines.

For all its persistence, the custom of Man eating Man (and *vice versa*) has never become really common either. One problem is that widespread enthusiasm for the practice tends to be self-limiting, if not self-extinguishing. Another is that if the enthusiasm doesn't infect the intended donors, their uncoöperative behavior leads to no end of wrangling and bitterness. And then there is the problem of disease.

Now, lumberjacks catch neither the Chestnut Blight nor the Dutch Elm Disease. Lobstermen are likewise immune to the ills that afflict their crustacean prey. But some diseases of poultry can be caught by their keepers; and with mammalian livestock, matters are much worse. When Man is both predator and prey, *everything* is catching, from the Common Cold on up to the Black Plague even before the donor is dispatched, along with a variety of aliments which can be ingested with the meal itself.

Some, like Tuberculosis, are quite rare, especially if one exercises reasonable care in selecting one's prey. Hepatitis is more common; more difficult to detect without an elaborate routine of testing and questioning of the donor, which tends to alarm him prematurely; and in the case of some virulent strains, almost impossible to destroy without burning the meat to a cinder and sometimes not even then. As for Trichinosis, one study has shown about a 2% infestation of pork and a 20% infestation of people. In theory, one could limit one's diet to devout Buddhists and Orthodox Jews; in practice, however, one can never be sure that the donor isn't a late convert. The usual precaution is simply to cook Man very thoroughly, as with pork only more so.

Happily, science has greatly reduced the risk of encountering these and other diseases in one's prey. Unfortunately, scientists have gone and introduced entirely new hazards of their own: the apparently clean-living, corn-fed youth from the farm is probably awash with DDT and the like from his work, while the magnificently muscled bodybuilder may be taking the same growth hormones which are no longer legal for raising beef and pork.

Of the various motives *for* eating Man, the most respectable is usually simple hunger. However, while Man is a nutritionally balanced food for Man—provided of course that the organs are eaten as well as the steaks and roasts—this is not entirely so when both eater and eaten are at the point of actual starvation. A sudden surfeit of lean meat on top of a severe deficiency of fats, oils, and essential vitamins can cause what is loosely called protein poisoning, which is one of the things that has given anthropophagy a bad name.

A second motive for eating people is to dispose of evidence. It is quite impossible to even estimate the frequency of application, since if done deftly, it will never be noticed. The best description of the procedure is the classic and—one hopes—wholly fictional short story, "Two Bottles of Relish," written by Lord Dunsany about 40 years ago; it has appeared in innumerable mystery anthologies since.

Other motives involve religion and magic, usually traceable to a desire to make *sure* that someone is *really* dead or to incorporate some of his virtues. (The contradiction implied by the *Old Testament* dietary laws and the symbolic anthropophagy of the *New* is beyond the scope of this study, however.) One could also cite the high cost of meat, but then, meat is *always* expensive. Another motive, simply liking the taste of Man, may be of limited significance; again, if deftly done, it would hardly come to public notice. A related situation is described in Damon Knight's celebrated short story, "To Serve Man," which was first published just 25 years ago and anthologized many times since.

In general, then, the practice of eating Man seems to be controlled by what economists call an "inelastic demand," which is to say that none of the laws cited above, nor social disapproval, nor even the vigorous objections of most donors has completely extinguished the custom. On the other hand, one cannot expect that this book will make the practice more common. The author, therefore, only hopes that publication of these recipes will make it more likely that when cannibalism does break out again, at least it will be done tastefully.

Timing is critical to successful preparation. There is nothing as wasteful as letting someone spoil while the survivors of a party of castaways debate whether or not they'll be rescued before they have to eat him. It is almost as bad to put off drawing lots for dinner until both diners and donor are too starved to do each other justice. On the other hand, it is quite embarrassing for the rescue party to arrive just as someone is served as dinner. In such a case, one can only invite the rescuers to share the meal and hope that they are more hungry than curious. Almost as bad is a visit from the local sheriff when evidence is about to be eaten; again, invite the visitor to dinner and hope. However, if inconvenient visitors are not apt to be a problem, then one can put by whatever can't be eaten at one sitting.

Man can be refrigerated, frozen, salted, and smoked. Drying, as Pemmican (*which see*) or Jerky, is possible but requires more work. Organ meats should be eaten promptly while the muscle, which keeps better, is saved for later. (Waste not, want not.) Briefly, meat to be frozen should be cut up, portions wrapped individually; and the freezer—unless very large—should be filled one layer at a time, allowing about an hour between layers to permit quick and solid freezing to about -20 degrees F. After the last layer has frozen, hold the whole load at that temperature for 24 hours, and then set the freezer to about 0 degrees F.

To salt—for example—60 pounds of meat, mix 5 pounds of non-iodized salt, 1-1/2 pounds of brown sugar, and 1 ounce saltpeter; or use 6 to 7 pounds of a commercially prepared dry cure mix. Use about half this quantity to coat each piece of meat. Pack the meat in a barrel and hold as close to 38 degrees F as possible. Keep for a week, then unpack, re-salt with the balance of the mixture, and pack again in the barrel. Total curing time should be 25 days or 3 days per pound of the largest piece, whichever is longer. More detailed instructions, including curing in brine, may be found in publications of the U.S. Department of Agriculture and the Morton Salt Company. Ask for their booklets on curing pork, as they will become unduly alarmed if they find out what you are really up to.

To smoke Man, begin with meat which has been salted and cured, as described above. Hang the pieces—not touching each other—in a small smoke-house or a large box to which the smoke from a small, slow-burning hardwood fire is piped. The temperature should be 90 to 110 degrees F; and smoking should continue as uninterruptedly as possible for 3 to 20 days, depending on the results one wants.

The question, upon whom should anthropophagy by practiced, is usually answered in terms of availability: one eats whoever is *there*. But, if there *is* a choice, it should be made with care, following the principle of getting the best specimen one can catch. After all, the legal complications cited above are assessed per capita rather than per pound; and the work to prepare a 97 pound beach-comber for table isn't much less than that required for a 220 pound graduate of a mail-order body-building course.

Contrary to folklore on the subject, children should be strictly avoided. They are small. Their disappearance sets off persistent, nosy search parties. They don't even taste good. There are drawbacks with women as well: they weigh less than men, on the average; and a lower percentage of that weight is muscle. They are less likely to be members of exploring parties that get in trouble than men are (men claim it's because the women have more sense; women say it's because the men won't let them go along). Finally, *To Serve Woman* is not the title of *this* book.

Therefore, except for a few stray lady wrestlers, the preferred donor for the cannibal table is a man who has reached his full growth but has not yet gone to fat or dried up with age. Since even a moderate spare tire represents a ridiculous quantity of lard, a lean, hard-muscled build is preferable to mere bulk. Football linemen are best toward the end of the season, when they've worked off excess weight. Athletes who have to diet down to a particular weight class, such as real (as opposed to TV) wrestlers and weightlifters, are excellent. Bodybuilders are ideal, especially in the larger sizes, although they are difficult to come by.

Of course, no end of misunderstandings can occur during the process of selecting a donor, especially when the selector and selectee are of the same gender. In such a case, the prospect may be even more wary than if he knew the true motives for the examination; but trying to explain will just make things worse. Since the ideal donor is precisely the one that can most effectively defend himself from incorporation, the whole process is pretty much a sporting proposition for everyone involved.

Things may be easier in the future. With large corporations taking over teams of professional athletes and the equally rapid penetration of those same corporations by the Mafia and other quasi-legal organizations, one may soon see some brutally direct action to resolve that old problem of the athlete whose performance falls below that upon which his contract salary was based. When this becomes common, groups of anthropophages can offer the managements of athletic teams an ecologically sounder means of disposal than the traditional ones of unlicensed cemeteries and concrete footwear, perhaps for a small handling fee of so much per capita or per pound.

Until that time, however, the pursuit of ideal or near-ideal donors will be a very chancy affair. This is not entirely a bad thing. Just as duck hunters take justifiable pride in shooting their prey on the wing rather than on the water, so too is there a virtuous thrill in trying to take someone who has the strength and skill to prey right back. Therefore, to be entirely sporting about it all, leave a copy of this volume in a prominent place in your kitchen, so that, if things do go awry, at least your intended quarry may do you as tastefully as you intended to do him.

OLD STANDBYS

Throughout these recipes for Person—roasted, boiled, baked, and broiled—and especially those with ground Man, one may substitute cubebs for pepper. Hyssop is another spice that goes well with Man, but must be used sparingly. For "cooking oil," use vegetable oil, margarine, butter, or lard made from whomever is to be cooked in it.

STEAKS, CHOPS, & ROASTS

With steaks, chops, and roasts we are on delicate ground. Steak is the all-American favorite—when an American tells you he has had a good meal, it's always steak—with prime rib roast not far behind. The finest Person-meat should be prepared as these cuts. But, since these cuts are so often served rare, with little in the way of added flavors or disguises, they are precisely the cuts most apt to distress squeamish eaters. Brasher folk, people who can ingest Basque Blood Soup, Animelles, or Chitterlings (*all of which see*) without blinking, won't be bothered, of course; but such eaters must always be the minority. Generally speaking, then, the cook should disregard the Tarzanian dictum, "Cooked meat is spoiled meat," and cook Person chops, roasts, and steaks until at least medium if not well done. For roasts, figure about 40 minutes per pound or use a meat thermometer and cook until internal temperature reaches 185 degrees F. Steaks are best *au poivre* or with a sauce. Marchand de Vin is excellent; and so are Bordelaise, Mushroom Sauce, and Sauce Trianon.

Serve Roast Person with Yorkshire Pudding and pan gravy or present it garnished with mounds of cooked vegetables (mushrooms, green peas, cauliflower, etc.) and with a gravy boat of Horseradish Sauce or Mushroom Sauce on the side. The same sauces may be used with chops. Rib chops are nice Frenched and with the end of the rib bone decorated with a stuffed olive or a curly paper frill. The aim here, as with all these dishes, is to veil from the diner that what he is eating went on two legs instead of four.

A last admonition: *don't* serve Person steaks for breakfast, even with a sauce. This is especially important if you served Man for dinner the night before. Breakfast comes at a queasy time of day. Lightly buttered toast, or toasted English muffins with marmalade would be a better choice. Black coffee and orange juice, please.

STEAK & OYSTERS

Even steak can get tiresome, especially when there is a couple of weeks' supply on hand. Here is an interesting variation.

> **3 pounds of Person steaks, about 1-1/2 inches
>   thick**
> **1 pint of oysters**
> **Salt, used sparingly**
> **Pepper**
> **Paprika**

Broil steaks 3 minutes to a side, remove from heat. Salt and pepper them to taste, cover with oysters, and sprinkle paprika with a generous hand. Bake in a 350 degree F oven until oysters are plump, about 5 minutes. Serve immediately. For 6.

BOILED LEG OF MAN

The kind of donor that we have suggested to be a practical compromise between availability and perfection should run about 20 pounds or so per thigh, about 7 per lower leg, while an exuberantly over-muscled specimen may provide thighs of as much as 30 pounds weight. Since people tend to be longer in the leg than—say—pork of the same weight, finding a big enough kettle to hold a whole thigh is not easy, though an old-fashioned wash boiler will do nicely, and the leftovers, afterwards, will seem to go on forever, unless one has an unusually hungry horde at table. If all difficulties are overcome, then:

Leg of Man
Whole cloves
Cracker crumbs
Brown sugar

Soak thigh or lower leg several hours in cold water. Scrub thoroughly. Put in kettle with water to cover and boil gently: lower leg, 4 hours; thigh, 5 to 6 hours (if at all possible, test with a meat thermometer to ensure internal temperature has reached 185 degrees F). Cool until it can be handled, remove skin, sprinkle with cracker crumbs and sugar, stick with whole cloves about 1 inch apart. Bake 90 minutes in a 300 degree F oven; serve hot or cold; allow about 1/2 pound per member of the hungry horde.

PERSON KEBAB

Spit-roasting is not only an interesting variation on conventional kitchen recipes, but it is also a very practical way to prepare Man under emergency conditions—such as being cast away or running out of food in the wilderness. It has been calculated that a 12-man party with nothing to eat but each other, with careful management, even under strenuous conditions, will take as long as 60 days to reduce to 3 reasonably well-fed survivors. In that length of time, they should be able to hike about a thousand miles or so, thus being virtually certain to find *some* kind of civilization. The recipe below, however, assumes more of a back-yard or picnic atmosphere than that:

3 pounds of Man, shoulder or pectoral muscle
 preferred, in 1 inch cubes
8 to 10 large mushroom caps
8 to 10 pieces of sweet bell pepper
8 to 10 large pineapple squares
—Marinade—
1/2 cup lemon juice
1 clove garlic, crushed
1/2 cup olive oil

Marinate cubed meat for at least 3 hours. Drain marinade and reserve. Thread meat on skewers, alternating meat, vegetables, and pineapple. While broiling 15 minutes, about 4 inches from coals, baste with a mixture of the reserved marinade, 1/3 cup honey, and 1/2 cup Worcestershire sauce. Turn frequently; serve on skewers. Some cooks argue that the meat and vegetables should be cooked separately, being careful to space meat cubes about an inch apart on skewers, to prevent the meat from getting soggy where in contact with the vegetable or pineapple; they may be re-skewered in alternating chunks just before serving. Other vegetable combinations are tomatoes and mushrooms, potatoes and mushrooms, and small onions with either. Whatever is used should be in pieces no larger than 1 inch in size. Other marinades may be made of 1 cup oil, 1/2 cup vinegar, 1/4 cup lemon juice, and spices; or of 2 cups red wine, 1/2 cup oil, and spices; or (for an unusual twist) 1/4 cup lemon juice, 1/4 cup oil, and 1 cup beer.

SHEPHERD'S PIE

This old fashioned, "cook-until-done" recipe was invented *for* shepherds, rather than to be made *of* them, although it might have some applicability to cattlemen's and sheepmen's feuds (*see also* Texas Chili with Cowboy). Whatever the applicability to range wars, it *has* proved excellent with left-over weight-lifter.

> **Cooked, left-over meat, cubed**
> **Cooking oil**
> **Mashed potatoes**
> **Salt**
> **Pepper**
> **Finely chopped onion**

Take enough meat to 3/4 fill a baking dish. Grease dish with cooking oil. Put one layer of mashed potato in the bottom of dish. Season meat, add onion, then put in dish. Top all with another layer of mashed potato. Bake at 400 degrees F until done.

PERSON PIE

Even more difficult than the task of finding a willing donor for the meat pie is that of finding pie plates of the proper size and shape. The result is indistinguishable from what is labeled "Pork Pie" and sold in British Railway stations, leading to suspicions that are doubtless without foundation. Or, so one hopes.

About 3 pounds bone and gristle
2 pounds ground Person
1/2 tsp. sage
1 tsp. salt
1/4 tsp. pepper
1 medium onion, chopped
2 cups pie crust mix, standard recipe or packaged, prepared according to its directions

Obtain pie plates, cylindrical in shape, about 3 inches in diameter, 2 inches high, a total of 8. Boil bones and gristle in 3 cups of water; continue boiling until liquid is reduced to 1 cup; strain, and reserve liquid. Prepare pie crust mix and line pie plates, reserving enough to cover each later. Mix ground Person, sage, salt, pepper, and reserved stock from bones; simmer 35 minutes in a skillet. Add onion, simmer 35 minutes more. Divide meat among pie plates, cover each with a circle of pie crust mix which has a hole in the center. Bake in a pre-heated oven at 450 degrees F until pie crust is lightly browned. Serve chilled or at room temperature. For 4 to 8.

MINCEMAN

While Minceman is tasty and stores well, a little meat produces an awful lot of pie filling. The recipe below should produce enough for about 16 pies, depending on the size of each.

4 pounds chopped Man, lean meat
2 pounds chopped Man, fat meat
2-1/2 pounds sugar
1-1/2 cups molasses
3 pints cider
3 pounds seeded raisins
2 pounds currants
1/2 pound citron, chopped fine
3 quinces, chopped
1-1/2 pounds apples, chopped
1-1/2 pints brandy
2 tsp. cinnamon
2 tsp. mace
2 tsp. ground cloves
1 tsp. nutmeg
3/4 tsp. pepper
1-1/2 tsp. salt, or to taste

Add just enough boiling water to cover the meat and cook until tender. Add sugar, molasses, cider, raisins, currants, citron, quinces, and apples; simmer gently for 120 minutes, stirring from time to time. Add brandy, cinnamon, mace, cloves, nutmeg, pepper, and salt; pour into jars, and seal. Makes about 2 gallons. For pies, make up any standard pie-crust mixture; line pie pan, fill with Minceman mixture (about 1 pint for a 9 inch pie), cover with pie-crust. Bake in 425 degree F oven for about 40 minutes and serve hot.

MAN-LOAF

Once basic Meat-Loaf has been mastered, this recipe becomes the starting point for an almost infinite set of variations. Of the standard ways to use ground Man—which also include Chili and Sausage, covered elsewhere in this work, and Manburger, which is too well-known to require special instructions—Man-Loaf, because of this flexibility, is best adapted to the problem of a fortnight or so of leftovers.

—Meat—
3 pounds ground Man
—Eggs—
2 eggs, lightly beaten
—Something dry—
1 cup cracker, toast, or bread crumbs; or quick-cooking barley; or 1/2 cup rice, pre-soaked 1 hour in 1 cup of water; or grated potato
—Seasonings—
2 tsp. salt, to taste
1/2 tsp. pepper, to taste
Perhaps 2 tsp. chopped onion or chives
Maybe 1 green pepper, chopped
If desired, 2 to 4 tsp. catsup
Or 4 tsp. Worcestershire sauce
Or even 1/2 tsp. sage, basil, or ground ginger
—And extra liquid—
1 to 2 cups milk, soup stock, tomato juice, or water

Mix all ingredients *except* spices thoroughly. Spread out mixture on a clean surface; sprinkle spices over mixture, fold, fold again, and shape into loaf. Bake 90 minutes covered, 30 minutes uncovered, in a 350 degree F oven. Serve hot or cold. For 6 to 8. *Be sure that the loaf has cooked all the way through; if the center is not done, return to oven until the meat has lost its redness.*

SCRAPPLE OF MAN

Whereas Haggis is made from organ meat and cereal and is associated with Scotland, Scrapple is of muscle meat—and cereal—and is a Philadelphia favorite. Either, without cereal, in aspic, is called Head Cheese. For Scrapple, then:

> **Meat scraps, trimmings, and other lean meat**
> **—Per pound of meat—**
> **1-1/2 cup water or stock in which the scraps**
>   **have been cooked**
> **1 tbsp. chopped onion**
> **4 oz. cornmeal or buckwheat flour**
> **1 tsp. salt**
> **1/2 tsp. pepper**
> **1/2 tsp. sage**
> **1/2 tsp. sweet marjoram**

Cook scraps in just enough water to cover for 2 hours; if meat-covered bones, joints, and so on are included, cook until meat falls from the bones. Drain, reserving stock. Grind coarsely after picking meat from bones. Weigh meat to establish quantities of other ingredients to add. Put stock in upper part of a double boiler (a large, heavy kettle can be used, but this requires constant stirring and a very low heat). Dampen flour or cornmeal and add to stock. Add meat, and cook for 45 minutes. Add rest of ingredients, and cook 5 minutes more. Pack into rectangular pans and chill. To serve, slice in 1/2 inch thick slices and fry in its own fat until brown. Use with maple syrup.

SAUSAGE

After the donor has been divided up into steaks, chops, and roasts, the leftover scraps of meat may be as much as half the total yield. While making sausage is a good way to use some of these odds and ends, don't go overboard and use too much of him in this recipe, lest appetite wane before the sausage does.

> Meat scraps, either 2/3 lean and 1/3 fat or 3/4 lean and 1/4 fat
> —Per pound of meat—
> For mild sausage:
> 1 tsp. salt
> 1/2 tsp. sage
> 1/2 tsp. pepper
> Or, for spicy sausage:
> 1 tsp. salt
> 1 tsp. sage
> 1 tsp. pepper

1/4 tsp. ground cloves or cumin
  Or, use a prepared seasoning mix

Chill meat overnight. Grind coarsely with seasonings. For a finer grain, chill and grind again with finer setting. Make into patties for immediate use, or stuff into casings, being careful to eliminate air pockets; then rub outside of casings liberally with dry curing salt. For longer storage, use meat which has been cured, as described elsewhere in this volume, make patties, fry partially, pack tightly into a sterilized crock, fill the crock to the brim with lard, and cover it tightly.

SUMMER SAUSAGE

This recipe is of questionable utility. For one, there isn't all that much need for extended storage, since the two principal reasons for eating somebody are to get rid of evidence or to fill a desperate need for meat. For another, the ever-present risk of trichinous meat dictates a time-consuming period of cold storage. However, in the interest of being complete . . .

Lean meat scraps
—Per pound of meat—
4 tsp. salt
1 tsp. sugar
1/2 tsp. sage
1/2 tsp. pepper
1/4 tsp. garlic powder

Hold meat scraps at 5 degrees F or colder for not less than 20 days. Thaw, mix with spices, grind twice. Spread on a dry, well-scrubbed surface or on waxed paper in a cool, *dry* location, screened from insects, for about 4 days. Stuff into casings, being sure that stuffed casings are flattened to not more than 3/4 inch thick. Rub surface liberally with 4 parts dry curing salt and 1 part dry sugar. Hang up to age; store in cool, dry place. Smoking is recommended.

SPAGHETTI SAUCE

This is another standard, classic recipe, though rather heavy on the meat since when cooking Man, there are so *many* leftovers. Incidentally, the reason that oregano is used so heavily in this and many other Italian recipes is that, given the right climate, the stuff grows so fast that it would otherwise take over every kitchen garden in the Mediterranean basin and most of those in California as well.

> **3 pounds ground Man**
> **1 tbsp. cooking oil**
> **1 medium onion, chopped coarsely**
> **2 cloves garlic**
> **12 oz. tomato paste**
> **4 cups tomatoes, cooked or fresh**
> **1/2 cup chopped parsley**
> **1 tbsp. sugar**
> **2 tsp. salt**
> **1 tsp. pepper**
> **1/4 tsp. sweet basil**

1 tsp. oregano
1/4 tsp. thyme
Cayenne or tabasco sauce, if desired

Crush garlic in a garlic press. Brown onion and garlic with cooking oil in a deep skillet. Add remainder of the ingredients, mixing thoroughly. (If using fresh tomatoes, peel and slice, and add 1 cup of water to the mixture.) Simmer all over very low heat for 90 to 120 minutes, stirring and adding water as needed; the sauce should be both smooth and thick. Refrigerate for 24 hours before re-heating and serving over any appropriate pasta—spaghetti, lasagne, et cetera. For 6 to 10.

PERSON PEMMICAN

For this preparation, the same precaution used for Summer Sausage should be taken if at all possible; if not, one must take one's chances.

Cut lean meat into thin, narrow strips. Dry completely in the sun or in a very slow oven. Grind and pound in a mortar with raisins or other dried fruits. Add hot lard of Man and knead into small cakes. Will keep indefinitely if kept dry and—if possible—cool.

BREAST OF MAN

No, this is not a recipe for preparing top-heavy ladies' salient features; the cut referred to here is the pectoral muscle with its underlying ribs. The other ribs can be used for Spareribs, *which see,* or for soups.

> 1 breast of Man, divided at the sternum
> 1 tsp. oregano
> 1 tsp. basil
> 1 tsp. ground cloves
> 2 tsp. salt, or to taste
> 1 tsp. pepper, or to taste
> 2 eggs, lightly beaten
> 1/2 cup flour
> 1/2 cup cracker crumbs
> 1 cup cooking oil

Place the divided sections in water to cover with oregano, basil, cloves, and pepper; simmer until the ribs can be removed easily—about 2 hours. Drain, remove bones, roll in flour, eggs, and salted cracker crumbs. Fry in hot oil, and serve hot. For 6 to 10; this cut of meat varies so much with different muscularity that matching donor to appetites is quite tricky.

TO SERVE MAN

ETHNIC DISHES

Anyone who has tried to disguise the leftovers from a large turkey served to a small family has but the beginnings of an idea of the problem posed by even a medium-sized body-builder and the leftovers from *him*. This varied set of recipes can perhaps help to cope. One must, however, be careful with some of the more highly spiced dishes described below, lest the diners be burnt more than the dinner.

HOMME BOURGUIGON

There are few things worse than using a poor grade "cooking" wine for a splendid dish such as this one. However, arguments by prospective donors that they be let at the wine beforehand should be firmly resisted, as it does no good if applied before the donor has been cubed.

3 pounds Person, lean meat, in 2 inch cubes
2 tsp. cooking oil
6 small onions, sliced
3 tbsp. flour
2 cups *good* Burgundy
1 cup white stock
1/2 pound small mushrooms, sliced
1 sprig parsley
1/4 tsp. thyme
1 bay leaf
1 clove garlic
1/2 tsp. salt, or to taste
1/4 tsp. pepper, or to taste

Marinate meat in Burgundy, stock, and spices for 4 hours, turning meat every 30 minutes. Remove meat, reserve marinade. In a heavy skillet, brown onions with cooking oil, remove onions and reserve. Brown meat in same skillet. Add flour, sprinkling lightly and turning meat, still browning. Add marinade, bring to a boil, cover, and simmer 2 hours. Return onions to skillet, add mushrooms, and simmer, covered, 1 hour more. Serve immediately. For 6.

PERSON STROGANOFF

One problem with Stroganoff is that the different ingredients have substantially different cooking times and should be cooked separately; accordingly, one should be prepared with two skillets, preferably heavy ones that hold the heat well. Because of the extraordinary variability in cooking time for different cuts of Person and even the same cut from different persons, it is well to test-cook a couple of pieces of the meat to determine the best time.

> 3 pounds Person, a good, lean cut, in strips
>   about 3 inches by 1 by 1/4
> 15 very large mushroom caps
> 1 medium onion, chopped coarsely
> 4 tbsp. butter
> 1 tsp. salt, or to taste
> 1/4 tsp. pepper, or to taste
> 1 cup sour cream
> —Optional but desirable—
> 3 to 6 oz. tomato paste
> 1/2 tsp. dry mustard
> 1 tsp. lemon juice

Sauté mushrooms until just done, about 5 minutes, and set aside covered. (Add tomato paste and mustard, if used, to this skillet.) In a second skillet, cook meat gently in just enough butter (meat may provide more fat as it cooks) until tender, which may be as little as 5 or as much as 15 minutes. Season with salt and pepper, stir in contents of first skillet. (Add lemon juice if used; flour may be used to thicken.) Add sour cream, heat just short of a boil, and serve immediately with rice. For 5.

HUNGARIAN GHOULASH

Imported paprika is absolutely necessary for a successful Hungarian Ghoulash, since the domestic version tends to be hopelessly bland. A good violinist or two can improve the flavor even more—but as players, not participants, for violinists are not noted for massive muscularity.

> 3 pounds lean Man, in 1 to 2 inch cubes
> 2 tsp. cooking oil
> 1 large onion, chopped coarsely
> 1 clove garlic
> 3 tbsp. flour
> 3 tsp. paprika
> 1 pint brown stock
> 1 pint Burgundy
> (Optional: 2 sweet red peppers, chopped; and
>   2 medium tomatoes, peeled and cubed)
> 1 bay leaf
> 1 tsp. salt, or to taste

Brown meat in heavy skillet with cooking oil. Add onion, and brown. Add flour, bay leaf, paprika; crush garlic in press, and add it. Stir in stock, wine, (and sweet peppers and tomatoes, if used), and bring to boil. Simmer covered for 2 hours or until tender; if heat is low enough, adding water will not' be necessary. Salt lightly to taste, serve with rice or boiled potatoes. For 6 to 8.

MANNERSCHNITZEL

There are few recipes better adapted to Man than the classical Schnitzel:

> 2 pounds of Man, cut across the grain in 1/2 inch slices
> 1 anchovy and 2 thin lemon slices per slice of Man
> 1 cup dry bread crumbs
> 1/2 cup flour
> 1 tsp. salt
> 1 tsp. pepper
> 1/2 tsp. sweet basil, ground
> 3 eggs, lightly beaten
> 1/2 cup cooking oil

Pound the sliced Man until 1/4 inch thick; immerse in water to cover, bring to a boil, and simmer 40 minutes or until tender. Reserve water for stock. Dip cutlets in flour, which has been seasoned with salt, pepper, and basil. Then dip cutlets in egg, then in bread crumbs. Chill. Heat oil in large skillet. Brown cutlets individually, then sauté together about 15 minutes. Remove, garnish with lemon slices and anchovies. Serves 6 to 8.

MENSCHLICHE SAUERBRATEN

This is not a spur-of-the-moment dish, but requires 3 days' preparation, not counting the time to gather the ingredients, select the donor, and so on.

> 6 pounds of Person, in 1 inch thick slices
> 2 cups wine vinegar
> 1 cup good red wine
> 4 tsp. salt
> 12 whole peppercorns
> 6 tsp. sugar (only 4 if a sweet wine is used)
> 3 bay leaves
> 12 whole cloves
> 2 tsp. mustard seeds
> 1/4 cup flour (or 1/4 cup gingersnap crumbs)
> 1 cup thick sour cream
> 1 tsp. salt, to taste
> 1 or 2 tsp. cooking oil

Put meat in covered glass or ceramic dish with all other ingredients except the flour and sour cream. Add just enough water to cover, if necessary; keep in a cool place for 3 days, turning meat each morning and evening. Remove meat, reserving marinade, dry with paper towels, dust well with flour, and brown it well, in a lightly greased skillet, both sides of each slice. Add 1 cup of the marinade, including a portion of peppercorns, bay leaves, and so on. Simmer 4 hours, adding marinade as needed. Strain 1 cup of marinade, skim, stir in sour cream, heat just short of a boil, and serve on the meat with potato dumplings. For 10.

GERMAN MEAT PIE

Here is a Teutonic way to serve leftover roast Man with manburger:

> 1 pound ground Man, lean
> 1/2 pound Man, pre-cooked and sliced
> 2 tsp. chopped chives
> 1 tsp. sweet basil
> 1 tbsp. Worcestershire sauce
> 1/2 tsp. salt
> 1/4 tsp. pepper
> 3 eggs, separated
> 2 cups pie crust mixture

Roll out half of the pie crust mixture (which may be any standard recipe or a packaged, prepared mix) and use it to line a 9 inch pie plate. Spread half of the sliced Man out on the bottom. Mix half of the egg yolks with the ground Man and the seasonings. Beat all of the egg whites and fold into this mixture, add remainder of sliced Man, place in pie plate. Cover with a 10 inch circle of pie crust mix, sealing the edges with some of the remaining egg yolk. Form the balance of the pie crust mix into strips and criss-cross them decoratively on top of the pie, sealing and glazing with the balance of the egg yolk. Bake for 1 hour in a 375 degree F oven. For 2 or 3.

MENSCHFLEISH KREPLACH,
KOSHER STYLE

Kreplach is sort of a Jewish won-ton (which can be defined as Chinese ravioli [which, of course, is a kind of Italian Kreplach]). However, since man-flesh is incurably *treife,* there *is* no such thing as Kosher Menschfleish Kreplach. Sorry.

PERSON WITH OYSTER SAUCE

Although Chinese recipes are easily adapted to anthropophagy, one should not assume that an interesting but unidentifiable dish in a Chinese restaurant is Shanghaied passer-by, since the Chinese feel that Occidentals are not worth eating and that

their fellow-Orientals are too worthy to eat—a pity, since the item below deserves wider circulation.

3 pounds of Person
2 tsp. ground ginger
1/4 cup cornstarch
2 tsp. sugar
1/2 to 1 cup oyster sauce
1/2 cup cooking oil
2 cups white stock
—Marinade—
1/4 cup sherry
2 tbsp. cornstarch
1 tbsp. sugar
Pepper to taste

Slice meat about 1/2 inch by 1 inch by 2; place in marinade for 60 to 120 minutes. Mix cornstarch with an equal volume of water (1/4 cup) and set aside. Heat a pan, add oil and ginger, turn up flame, add meat and fry for 3 minutes, stirring constantly. Add stock, bring to boil, reduce heat. Add cornstarch and water, sugar, oyster sauce, and cook until mixture thickens (about 3 to 6 minutes). Pepper to taste; serve with steamed rice. For 8 to 12.

SWEET & SOUR MAN

Or, more accurately, "Sweet and *Pungent* Man." There is a great deal of flexibility in the fruits and vegetables used with this recipe: almost any fruit juice may be substituted for the traditional orange in the sauce, provided that the proper balance of tartness and sweetness is maintained, and it is even possible to substitute marmalade or jam, though some careful adjustments to the amount of added sugar are necessary.

> 3 pounds of Man
> Cooking oil
> 2 tbsp. soy sauce
> 1 tsp. salt
> Cornstarch
> 2 cups of a mixture of pineapple chunks, sliced red sweet peppers, and carrots
> (Optional: 10 slices preserved ginger)
> —Sauce—
> 2 tbsp. sugar, or to taste
> 1 tbsp. vinegar
> 2 tbsp. cornstarch
> 2 tbsp. soy sauce
> 4 tsp. tomato paste
> 2 tbsp. red wine
> 4 tsp. orange juice
> 3 tbsp. water

Slice meat across the grain in 3/8 inch slices, then cut into oblongs, 3/4 by 1-1/2 inch in size. Marinate with salted soy sauce, turning occasionally, for 90 minutes, then coat with cornstarch, dampening further with soy sauce as needed. Deep-fry until crisp (oblongs should float when done), remove to drain on paper towels in a medium oven. Mix ingredients for the sauce (if one has any doubts as to the proportions of sweetness and tart, this should be done in advance), pour into lightly oiled pan, and bring to boil, stirring constantly. Add pineapple, red peppers, and carrot slices (proportions can be varied; total volume of all three should be about 2 cups), as well as ginger, if used. Cook 2 minutes more. Transfer fried oblongs of Man to a heated platter, pour on sauce, and serve at once, while meat is still hotter than the sauce. For 6 to 10.

CURRIED PERSON,

CANTONESE

The essence of much Chinese cooking is simple necessity; how does one prepare food when fuel is scarce? The Chinese solution—cut up everything in small pieces and avoid overcooking—characterizes many of their recipes, such as this one:

2 pounds Person, lean meat preferred
1 medium onion, chopped coarsely
3 tbsp. cornstarch
1 tsp. sugar
1 tsp. salt
1 to 3 tbsp. curry powder
1-1/2 cups brown stock

Mix cornstarch with an equal volume of water (3 tbsp.) Cut meat in strips, about 1/2 by 1/2 inches in cross section. Heat curry in a dry pan, stirring rapidly to keep from scorching. Add onion, then meat, still stirring, and cook for about 4 minutes over low flame, stirring continually. Add stock, sugar, and salt; bring to boil quickly, simmer, still stirring, for 4 minutes more. Add cornstarch and water, bring to boil once more, and serve hot, with steamed rice. For 4 to 6.

SPARERIBS, SHANGHAI STYLE

The name, oddly enough, has nothing to do with being extra or excess; it is taken from the German for "ribs (for the cooking) spit" and is properly applied to any ribs which naturally have, or have been trimmed to have, only a thin covering of meat. While in theory, ribs may simply be baked or fried, they tend to be pretty leathery cooked thus, and the results are much better if they are stewed first, as described below:

> **3 pounds ribs**
> **1/4 tsp. garlic powder**
> **1/2 tsp. ground ginger**
> **2 tsp. sugar**
> **3 tbsp. soy sauce**
> **3 tbsp. sherry**
> **1 cup brown stock**
> **Pepper to taste**
> **Cooking oil**

Ribs may be cut into sections about 3 inches by 4, or may be separated into individual ribs and cut to about 4 inch lengths. Rub ribs with ginger and garlic (1 clove of garlic, crushed in a garlic press, may be substituted for the garlic powder), and fry, stirring rapidly, for 4 minutes, in a deep skillet. Add stock, sugar, soy sauce, and sherry, bring to boil, cover, and simmer for 30 to 45 minutes, turning over twice in that time. Remove meat to a 350 degree F oven, on paper towels, for 9 to 15 minutes to crisp the outsides. Serve plain, with plum sauce, or covered with sauce from "Sweet and Sour" recipe above (make up 1/2 to 2/3 quantity of that sauce). For 3 to 8 as an appetizer.

WHITE CUT OF MAN

This dish is an exception to the Chinese habit, mentioned above, of cutting everything up beforehand. And no, the pigmentation of the donor has nothing to do with the color of this dish.

3 pounds of Man
Plum sauce
Chinese mustard

The calf or biceps are excellent for this recipe; place the meat, in one piece, in the lower part of a double boiler with water to cover and a lid. Bring to a boil and cook briskly for 6 minutes. Transfer meat and liquid to upper half of boiler, add water to lower half, place upper half of boiler in lower, and continue to cook, gently, for the balance of an hour. Remove boiler from heat, drain upper half and return it, with meat inside, to lower half. Let cool to room temperature with lid in place (about 1 hour). Cut into

3/8 inch slices, quarter the slices, and serve—arranged in an overlapping spiral on a large, round plate—with plum sauce and mustard (use the latter with caution; it is *hot!*). As an appetizer, for 12 to 25.

EAST INDIAN

CURRIED PERSON

Although the list of ingredients looks forbidding, the dish itself is fairly easy to prepare; the principal caution is to match the degree of seasoning to the tastes of the diners. It is a particularly good way to prepare meat for guests who might object if they knew whom they were eating.

> 3 pounds of Person, in 1 by 1/2 by 1/4 inch
> pieces
> 4 tsp. cooking oil
> 3 medium onions, chopped coarsely
> 2 cups thick sour cream
> —Any 2 of the 3 items below—
> 2 small apples, sliced
> 4 medium tomatoes, peeled and sliced
> 1/2 cup chopped celery
> —The 2 items below are optional—
> 1 tsp. brown sugar
> 1 clove garlic, crushed in a garlic press
> —Spices below are for a *hot* curry—
> 2 tsp. coriander
> 3/4 tsp. turmeric
> 3/4 tsp. cumin

3/4 tsp. chili powder
1/2 tsp. ground ginger
1/2 tsp. cinnamon
1/2 tsp. cardamom
1/2 tsp. mace or nutmeg
1/4 tsp. cayenne

For a milder curry, use half the indicated quantities for the spices "coriander" through "cayenne" above. Put these spices in a *dry* frying pan and heat, while stirring rapidly. When fragrance of curry is strong, add oil and onions, being careful not to let the curry burn. Fry onions gently for 3 minutes. Add meat and brown it. Add balance of ingredients (except cream), bring to a boil, and simmer very gently for 45 minutes (or transfer to a double boiler and cook for 50 minutes). Add sour cream, bring barely to a boil. Sprinkle with parsley, salt to taste; and serve with rice, grated coconut, chopped peanuts, raisins, and chutney. For 6.

TEXAS CHILI WITH COWBOY

Some argue that cowboy meat is too tough to be served any other way, especially since the spices tend to kill the taste of whatever the donor may have been smoking, drinking, or chewing. Others discount this argument, but agree that Chili is a practical, quick way to serve Man in well-disguised form.

Meat of 1 reasonably well-muscled Cowboy,
    ground coarsely
15 pounds onions, chopped
10 cloves garlic, crushed
1/2 cup cooking oil
25 pounds pre-cooked kidney beans
25 pounds fresh tomatoes
2 oz. salt
6 to 12 oz. chili powder
2 oz. sugar
1/2 oz. pepper, freshly ground
(Optional: 40 green bell peppers)
(Optional: 3 tsp. paprika)

On a frying grill or in a battery of skillets, brown onions, meat, and bell peppers (cut up) if used, for about 5 minutes per batch. Peel and quarter tomatoes. Put tomatoes, beans with their cooking water, and 2-1/2 gallons additional water in large kettle or wash boiler (or divide among several smaller ones). Add meat, onions, peppers if used, and seasonings. Simmer for 90 minutes; serve in bowls or with rice. For 150.

MEXICAN (REAL)

CHILI CON HOMBRE

Although there is much rivalry between Mexicans and Texans over their respective kinds of Chili, neither group seems at all willing to volunteer the requisite raw material for a proper study, so that researchers

must continue to make do with whomever they can catch.

> 3 pounds of Person, rump preferred, in 1/2 inch cubes
> 1 Spanish onion, chopped fine
> 6 *Ancho* chilies
> 1 clove garlic, chopped
> 1 tsp. cooking oil
> 1/2 tsp. oregano or cumin
> 1 tsp. salt, or to taste
> 1/2 tsp. pepper, or to taste
> 2 cups pre-cooked kidney beans

Put meat in kettle with just enough water to cover, bring to boil, and simmer covered for 1 hour. Remove stems, veins, and seeds from chilies and soak chilies in hot water for 1 hour, then drain and grind (or blend with an electric mixer) with onion and garlic. Oil a heavy skillet, heat, and add mixed chili, onion, and garlic; cook five minutes. Transfer to kettle with the rest of the spices, simmer all 1 additional hour. Add beans with water in which they were cooked, bring to boil, and simmer 15 minutes more. Serves 8 to 10.

MEXICAN
RED STEWED HOMBRE

And no, there is no special virtue in using Amerinds for this recipe. Do not attempt this dish with the so-called chili powder available in ordinary grocery stores; use only genuine *Ancho* chilies. No substitute will do at all.

> 3 **pounds lean meat of Man, in 2 inch pieces**
> 6 *Ancho* **chilies**
> 2 **small onions, chopped fine**
> 3 **whole cloves**
> 1 **clove garlic**
> 1/2 **tsp. oregano**
> 1/2 **tsp. cumin**
> 1 **tsp. brown sugar**
> 1/2 **pound fresh plum tomatoes, peeled and chopped**
> **Salt and pepper to taste**

Cover meat with boiling water with 1 onion and cloves; simmer for 2 hours, covered. From the chilies, carefully remove stems, veins, and seeds, and soak chilies in hot water to cover for 1 hour, then grind with cloves, garlic, oregano, and cumin; mix with second onion, tomatoes, sugar, and 1 cup of the water in which the meat has been simmering; and grind all together. (An electric blender, though hardly traditional, is of enormous help at this stage of the operation.) Heat this sauce in a large skillet, stirring constantly, for 5 minutes, drain meat, add to skillet, simmer at very low heat for 30 minutes, and serve. For 6.

MEXICAN

GREEN STEWED HOMBRE

Again, the real Mexican stews must be put off until there is a supply of *genuine* chilies of the proper kinds to hand. And it is better to cheat a little and use an electric blender rather than struggle with a mortar and pestle borrowed from the corner apothecary. (Of course, if you do this often, you *could* treat yourself to a mortar of your own.)

3 pounds lean meat of Man, in 2 inch pieces
3 *Ancho* chilies
3 *Jalapeño* chilies
2 small onions
1 clove garlic, chopped
6 Romaine lettuce leaves

1 small can, Mexican green tomatoes
1/2 tsp. coriander
1/2 cup orange juice
Salt and pepper to taste

Drop meat and 1 onion in boiling water to just cover and simmer, covered, for 2 hours. Remove seeds, veins, and stems from *Ancho* chilies, stems and seeds from *Jalapeño* chilies; soak together in hot water to cover for 1 hour. Grind together (or use blender on) chilies, the other onion, garlic (which may be crushed in a garlic press, if available), lettuce leaves, tomatoes with the juice from their can, and coriander. When mixture is smooth, bring to boil and simmer 5 minutes in a skillet, stirring constantly. Season to taste with salt and pepper, and add orange juice. Drain meat, pour sauce over it, and simmer at very low heat (use a double boiler if available) for 30 minutes more. Serve with rice. For 6.

LONG PIG, BAKED IN AN IMU

Select the location of the Imu with care; it must not be subject to flooding, for although it can stand being rained on, immersion is a disaster. The ground may be damp but must not be saturated. Sandy soil is best. Select and gather rocks of total volume twice that of the intended donor. These must be picked with some care, for they must withstand being heated red hot. Limestone, slate, and chalk are unusable. Granite, basalt, and quartzite—and volcanic rocks of all kinds —are good. Pumice—a porous, volcanic rock, which is very light in weight—is perfect. Ordinary fire-brick is almost as good. Test the rocks by heating a few red hot and then cooling slowly; if they survive mostly intact, gather more like those tested and dry them thoroughly with a moderate fire. Dig the Imu itself about 2 feet deep and about 2 feet longer and wider than the donor, piling the earth along the sides. Use about half the rocks to make a layer at the bottom of the pit. In the middle of this layer, build a pyramid of kindling and on that, a layer of 6 to 8 inch logs. Pile the remaining rocks on top of the pyramid, leaving some means to set the kindling alight after the rocks are in place. Start fire; in about 3 hours, the rocks should be red hot.

Prepare donor—remove head and innards, shave or singe off body hair, truss firmly to a couple of stout, sturdy poles—and stuff with hot rocks wrapped in banana, ti, or palm leaves or dampened corn husks. Pull the pile of rocks apart and spread out in a layer on the bottom of the pit. Cover stones with a thick layer of banana, ti, or palm leaves or dampened corn husks and stalks. Put in donor, lying on poles; cover with more leaves; cover all with burlap bags well soaked in water, then a dampened tarp or waterproof sheet. Pile dirt on top, dampen lightly, and cap any jets of escaping steam with more dirt. Keep watch for 6 to 8 hours, dampening dirt as it dries and covering steam vents as they develop, then uncover and unearth dinner. Vegetables can be cooked with the meat—yams are traditional, but Irish potatoes will do as well. Serves 60 to 90.

TO SERVE MAN

VARIETY MEATS

For all the traditional emphasis on steaks, chops, and roasts, the fact remains that the most nourishing parts of Person are the organ meats. This section, then, is of particular importance, as it gives directions for preparing parts which—of beef, mutton, and pork—are all too seldom seen on the table and which, therefore, are unfamiliar to most cooks.

HAGGIS

By ancient tradition, haggis is made of the innards of sheep, served with kilted ceremony and prolonged bagpiping in a drafty Scottish castle. Some music lovers claim that the haggis tastes much better without bagpipes; and to ensure quiet, they recommend substituting the piper for the sheep. Other Scots insist that anyone who cannot appreciate the stirrin' music o' th' pipes should be a participant in the menu rather than a partaker. In either case, the stomach of Man can not hold the rest of his internal plumbing as well as that of a sheep can its own (observations of hungry teenagers at table notwithstanding). Consequently, there may be more stuffing than the container can take in the following recipe; if

that happens, put the surplus in a double boiler or into sausage casings and cook it with the rest of the haggis.

Of 1 Man, the stomach, liver, heart, and lights
2 cups dry oatmeal
1 pound fat, chopped coarsely
2 medium onions, chopped
1 tsp. pepper
4 tsp. salt
1/2 tsp. nutmeg
2 tbsp. lemon juice
3 cups soup stock

Soak stomach several hours in salted water. Turn inside out (cut no more than necessary to accomplish this), scrub lining, and turn right side out again. Wash heart, liver, and lights (lungs), removing tubes and veins. Cover heart and lights with cold water, bring to boil, and simmer 45 minutes. Add liver, simmer 45 minutes more. Remove meat from water. Chop one half the liver coarsely; chop rest of liver and all of heart and lights very finely. Mix with fat, onions, spices, lemon juice, and enough of the stock to make a soft mixture. Stuff stomach, leaving room for oatmeal to swell, and sew up openings. Bring water to boil again, add rest of stock, and put in haggis. Trapped air will probably cause it to swell; prick a small hole to let air out if this happens. Simmer for 3 hours, remove to covered hot platter, let stand for 20 minutes, remove thread, slice, and serve. For 10 to 15.

EARS SEABRIGHT

It's the little extras and special touches that make the difference between an ordinary homicue and something that's out of this world.

For up to 6 pairs of ears:
1/2 medium onion, sliced
1/2 carrot, sliced
1/4 tsp. whole peppercorns
1 sprig parsley
1/2 bay leaf
1/2 tsp. salt

The night before the 'cue, separate ears from donors. Drop into a pan of cold water, add remainder of ingredients. Bring to a boil and cook until tender-crisp. On the day of the 'cue, wipe the ears dry, sprinkle with salt and pepper, and wrap each in aluminum foil. Broil over coals for 5 minutes. For a crisper tidbit, string directly on a skewer. Serve with prepared mustard. Delicious with beer.

BLOOD SAUSAGE

In theory, the 5 quarts of blood in a healthy man could be worth about $300. Unfortunately, blood banks have a firm rule about using only live donors—both before and after—so that in practice this potential cannot be fully realized. Even collecting for blood sausage is deceptively difficult, owing to the uncoöperative behavior of most donors; but there is usually enough for at least some of this delicacy when things finally settle down.

—**For each quart of blood—**
1 pound of meat scraps
Cornmeal as required
2 tbsp. salt
1-1/2 tsp. pepper
Chopped onion, mace, or ginger to taste

Stir fresh blood with a whisk, removing fibers as they form in the fluid. Cook meat scraps in just enough water to cover for 30 minutes, grind coarsely, and mix in seasonings. Stir this into the blood. Add cornmeal if necessary to give the mixture the thickness of hot cereal. Stuff the result in sausage casings. Bake in oven at 160 degrees F for 2 hours. The sausages may thereafter be smoked, or simply chilled until eaten.

LARD & CRACKLINGS

In these cholesterol-conscious times, good old-fashioned lard has fallen out of favor, which is a pity, for it is both tasty and digestible. Since the point of eating somebody is to *eat,* it makes no sense whatever to discard this portion of him; one can go on a diet some other day.

Fat of 1 Man
1 pinch baking soda

Cut fat, when cool, into small pieces. Place all in a large kettle with a little water in the bottom to prevent initial scorching. Add pinch of baking soda. Heat slowly, stirring frequently and watching constantly. Remove cracklings—small pieces of membrane and skin—as they rise to the top of the liquid lard, since if left they will eventually sink and then scorch on the bottom of the kettle. Drain cracklings; serve as an appetizer. Continue heating the lard until its temperature reaches 255 degrees F (do not guess; use a thermometer!), then reduce heat to maintain that temperature for 30 minutes to boil out all remaining water. Cool to about 150 degrees F, then pour into crocks that have been sterilized. Cover tightly and store in a cool, dry place. May be used wherever these recipes specify "cooking oil."

LIVER JEREMIAH

While raw liver *is* edible, the results are far tastier— and safer—if time is taken to prepare it properly. The following recipe is one such method, adaptable to wilderness conditions.

> 1 liver
> 2 pounds, more or less, of fat meat in thin
>   slabs
> 1 tsp. pepper
> 1/2 tsp. cayenne
> 1 tsp. sage
> 1 tsp. thyme

Divide liver into 6 equal parts. Sprinkle each with spices, then cover with a layer of fat meat, binding with string into roughly symmetrical shapes. Skewer and cook about 12 inches over a medium bed of coals for 20 minutes, or until another skewer, piercing the meat, no longer draws red or pink fluid. Remove from fire, unwrap fat, and return to fire for 3 to 6 minutes to brown the outside. Serve on skewers. For 3 to 6.

FRIED LIVER

The usual meat animals do not drink to excess. Man does, which is a pity, considering the amount of good liver that gets spoiled that way. While there are advantages in getting a prospective donor in a coöperative mood with liquid inducements (being careful not to use up the cooking sherry or the wines), avoid donors who drink on all other occasions as well.

> **Liver of 1 Man (about 4 to 5 pounds)**
> **1/4 pound scraps of fat meat**
> **1/2 pound scraps of lean meat**
> **1 small clove of garlic, minced**
> **1 tsp. salt, or to taste**
> **1/2 tsp. pepper, or to taste**

Wash liver, drain, and remove outside skin and major veins. Cut meat scraps into thin strips. Cut liver into 1/2 inch slices. Fry meat scraps in their own fat until lean meat is crisp, remove, and drain. Fry liver, about 2 or 3 minutes to a side, until the redness is just gone; do not overcook. Serve liver garnished with meat scraps. For 10.

KIDNEY & MUSCLE STEW

In Man, the kidneys weigh about 1/4 pound each. Unlike those of more ordinary meat animals, people's kidneys are sometimes subject to stones; careful inspection is necessary to keep from breaking a tooth on what should be a choice, tender morsel. The recipe that follows is a variation on a classic standard.

> **1 pair kidneys**
> **3 pounds lean Man, in 1 inch cubes**
> **2 tsp. cooking oil**

2 medium onions, chopped
2 tsp. vinegar
1 tbsp. red wine
Salt and pepper to taste

Wash kidney, remove tubes and fat, cut into 1/2 inch cubes. Put cooking oil with any fat from kidneys and meat in a deep skillet, add chopped onions, and sauté until brown. Add meat, 3 cups boiling water, vinegar, and wine. Cover and simmer until tender, about 90 minutes. Serve hot. For 6.

BAKED KIDNEY

This is a deceptively simple, yet choice dish, requiring only

1 pair kidneys, with covering fat intact

Wash kidneys, removing tubes and feeling carefully for possible stones. Place in a small, covered, well-greased baking dish; bake for 90 minutes at 325 degrees F. Remove fat, serve hot. For 2.

TONGUE

Remove, wash thoroughly. Put in boiling water to cover which has been seasoned with bay leaf, cloves, and peppercorns. Simmer 2 hours, remove, dip in cold water, and remove skin. Serve cold, sliced, with horseradish and mustard, as appetizer.

STEWED LIGHTS

Lights—or lungs—are not terribly popular, but it seems a shame to throw anything away, so . . .

Lights of 1 Man, in 2 inch cubes
1 medium onion, sliced
2 cloves garlic, chopped
1 stalk celery, chopped
1 cup cooked tomatoes
1/2 pound of potatoes, cubed
1/2 cup cider
1/2 tsp. sweet basil
1/2 tsp. salt, to taste
1 tbsp. cooking oil

Brown meat, onion, celery, and garlic with cooking oil in a deep skillet. Add cider and potatoes, cover, and simmer 30 minutes. Add tomatoes and basil, cover, and simmer 45 minutes or until tender. Salt to taste. Serves 4 to 6.

HEART & LUNG PAPRIKASH

Surely it is just a coincidence that paprika appears so often in these recipes for Man. After all, though paprika is certainly Hungarian, nowadays Transylvania is a part of Rumania. City lungs, however, may be too dark and gritty to be usable; corn-fed non-smokers are preferred here.

Of 1 Man, the heart and lungs
1/4 cup cooking oil
1 medium onion, chopped
4 cloves garlic, crushed in garlic press
3 tbsp. paprika (imported preferred)
2 tbsp. flour
2 cups soup stock
8 oz. tomato paste
1/4 cup lemon juice
1/4 cup chopped dill
4 tsp. brown sugar
1/2 tsp. salt, or to taste
1/4 tsp. pepper, or to taste

Remove fat and tubes from meat, cut into 1 to 2 inch cubes. Heat oil in a large skillet, add onion and garlic, and brown. Add meat, then cook until it turns color. Stir in flour and paprika, then stock, tomato paste, and lemon juice. Bring to a boil, then simmer, covered, for 90 to 150 minutes, until meat is tender. Add sugar and additional lemon juice, a little at a time, tasting to reach a sweet-sour flavor. Serve hot, garnished with dill. For 5 to 7.

STUFFED HEART

In theory volunteers would be expected to be tenderer here; in practice, the difference, if any, does not appear to be statistically significant.

1 heart (about 1/2 to 3/4 pound)
1/2 cup of any standard chestnut stuffing
   mixture
Salt and pepper to taste
1 cup Burgundy

Wash heart thoroughly and remove major veins. Slit open for stuffing. Place in Burgundy · overnight, turning twice. Remove and drain, reserving Burgundy. Stuff with stuffing and close the slit with a skewer. Place in a small covered baking dish, add Burgundy, and bake 120 minutes in a preheated 325 degree F oven, adding water as the Burgundy cooks away. Serves 2.

BRAINS

WITH MUSHROOM SAUCE

Exercise toughens or enlarges almost every part of Man except the brains, so those of a thinker are quite as tender as those of—well—whatever ethnic or occupational group one cares to insult. They are so tender—the brains, not the ethnic/occupational group—that they should be pre-cooked immediately they become available, as follows:

1 set brains (about 2-1/2 pounds)
2 tsp. salt
2 tsp. vinegar

Rinse gently in cold water, place in saucepan, cover with gently boiling water, add salt and vinegar, and simmer covered for 35 minutes.

1 set brains, pre-cooked as above
1 pint sherry
2 cups sliced mushrooms
2 cups cooked tomatoes
1/2 cup flour
1/4 cup cooking oil
1/2 tsp. salt
1/4 tsp. pepper
1/2 tsp. oregano

Cut pre-cooked brains into 1 inch cubes. Place in bowl, pour in sherry, and let stand 90 minutes. Sauté mushrooms. Add tomatoes and seasonings, bring to a boil, transfer sherry from bowl to sauce, and bring to boil again. Serve sauce hot, over the brains. For 6 to 9.

SAUTÉED BRAINS

Begin with pre-cooked brains, as above. In a skillet, fry in their own fat 1/4 pound sliced fat scraps and 1/2 pound lean sliced scraps; when crisp, remove and drain. Sauté brains in the hot oil until browned. Serve garnished with the scraps. For 5 to 8.

BAKED MELTS

Melts are spleens; people come equipped with one each. As with other internal plumbing, the melt must be used quickly, as it spoils easily.

1 melt (about 1/4 pound)
1 tbsp. cooking oil
Salt
Pepper
Tomato sauce

Soak the melt in cold water for 20 minutes. Remove veins and membranes. Parboil in lightly salted water and drain. Place in a small baking dish. Heat oil, pour over melt, then bake in a medium oven until nicely browned, and serve with salt, pepper, and tomato sauce.

SWEETBREAD

While the neck sweetbread—the thymus—in Man is disappointingly small, the one on the back of the abdominal cavity—the pancreas—is about 1/4 pound in weight.

1 sweetbread
1 tsp. salt
1 tsp. vinegar
1 or 2 tsp. cooking oil
Paprika

Bring 2 cups of water to boil, with salt and vinegar. Drop in sweetbread, simmer 15 minutes. Remove, drain, and discard veins and membranes. Brush with cooking oil; broil until nicely browned. Sprinkle liberally with paprika; serve in a hot dog roll.

CASINGS

Casings, for sausages and the like, are made of the upper intestine. (The lower intestine is one of the very few parts of Person which are discarded; and this should be done quickly and carefully, without spilling the contents.) The small intestine should be washed thoroughly, turned inside out, and the inside scraped thoroughly, several times. To invert the intestines, the trick is to hold a length vertically, form a cuff at the low end, and fill the cuff with water from a hose so that the weight of the water draws the rest down and around and inside out. Casings can be stored for a few days in dry curing salt.

CHITTERLINGS

This recipe has an ominous look to it—the potato is there solely to absorb various odors and flavors—but the results are not all *that* bad.

Small intestines of 1 Man
1 small potato
1-1/2 cups vinegar
2 tsp. salt
1 tsp. pepper
1 clove garlic
1/4 to 1/2 tsp. cayenne

Clean intestines thoroughly, as for Casings, above. Place in a large pot and add boiling water to cover.

Add 1 cup of vinegar, potato, and seasonings. Simmer, covered, for 3 hours. Discard potato. Remove Chitterlings, reserving liquid. Cut into 1 inch lengths, return to pot with just enough liquid to cover. Add 1/4 cup vinegar, simmer uncovered 20 minutes. Drain, pour on remaining 1/4 cup vinegar, and serve hot.

TONGUE-IN-CHEEK CHEESE

Of the two variants of head cheese listed here, this one is the spicier. If the hands or feet are omitted, reduce the other ingredients a suitable amount.

> **Head, hands, and feet of 1 Man**
> **2 quarts white wine**
> **2 large onions, quartered**
> **8 whole cloves**
> **Stick of cinnamon, 1 inch or more**
> **Extra large** *bouquet garni*
> **4 tsp. salt**
> **10 to 20 whole peppercorns**
> **4 tsp. celery salt**
> **1/4 tsp. cayenne**
> **1 tsp. nutmeg**
> **1/2 tsp. sage**
> **1/2 tsp. thyme**

Clean head, hands, and feet, removing all hair. Remove and reserve brains and tongue. Place head, hands, and feet in deep kettle, together with other available meat scraps if desired. Cover with wine, adding water as needed. Add onions, cloves, cinnamon, *bouquet garni,* salt, peppercorns, and celery salt. Bring to boil, simmer covered for 30 minutes. Skim, add tongue, re-cover, and simmer 2 hours. Remove tongue when tender, which should be at this time, and simmer rest 1 hour more, skimming as required. Add brains, simmer 15 minutes more. Remove all from water, reserving both. When cool, remove meat from bones and cut, including tongue, in small pieces. Peel membranes from brains and chop coarsely. Cut tongue into 1/2 inch cubes. Mix meat in large bowl, adding cayenne, nutmeg, sage, and thyme. Transfer to deep crock or rectangular pans, add stock (strained) to cover, affix lid, and refrigerate 2 to 4 days before serving, cold and sliced.

FOOT-IN-MOUTH CHEESE

This is a milder-tasting recipe than that above. It presupposes that the brains and tongue will be put to other uses. As before, if hands or feet are omitted, reduce other ingredients appropriately.

Of 1 Man, the head, hands, and feet
3 bay leaves
2 cloves garlic
1 tbsp. salt
1 tsp. pepper
2 tsp. thyme
2 tsp. sweet basil

Clean head, hands, and feet. Remove and dispose of hair. Remove for use elsewhere the tongue and brains. Place head, hands, and feet in a deep pot with remaining ingredients and water to cover. Bring to boil and simmer covered—skimming as required—until meat falls from the bones, which will take about 3 to 5 hours. Drain, reserving stock. Pick meat from bones and grind coarsely, seasoning further to taste if desired with ground cloves and coriander. Place in deep crock or rectangular pans, add strained stock until saturated, cover, and refrigerate 3 to 5 days. Serve cold, sliced.

GREBENES

While many people dislike skin on their roasts, others are devotees of the outer layer. For the latter, we suggest the following as a snack:

Skin, shaved, scraped, and cubed
1 large onion, chopped
Cooking oil

Fry the onion and skin until the skin is well crisped. Drain well on paper towels, sprinkle with salt, and serve like popcorn with beer, etc.

ANIMELLES

Also called "mountain oysters" or "fries," after a standard method of preparation, these organs are the subject of circumspection when being spoken of by most people, even when the donor is beef or mutton. Most cookbooks carefully ignore the whole region, and many otherwise openminded anthropophages insist on discarding the whole sexual apparatus— vitals, accessories, and all—as inedible. Only slightly less puritanical are those who toss the works into the meat grinder for the Haggis or Headcheese. On the other extreme are the really bizarre recipes (e.g. peel, proceed as for Blood Sausage with contents, re-stuff, and bake) which, however, are beyond the scope of this volume. Of some interest, then, is the following recipe for the (ahem) vitals, while the rest of the equipment can go in with the ground meat, et cetera.

> **1 pair of *Animelles***
> **Cooking oil**
> **Lemon wedge**
> **Salt and pepper to taste**

Wash organs in cold water. Remove covering membrane. Soak 30 minutes in lightly salted water. Cut into 1/4 inch slices. Fry gently in deep cooking oil until golden brown. Drain, season, and serve with lemon wedge.

SOUPS & STEWS

While Man, as a rule, is both tender and tasty, a few recalcitrant donors may turn out to be tough going when served broiled or roasted. Marinating is one solution for these individualists; stewing is another. Soups and stews are also useful in adding variety to the menu, in extracting the last bit of goodness from the donor's bony remnants, and—when the occasion arises—in preparing Person in a thoroughly well disguised form.

WHITE STOCK

These days, when people worry about racism even more than they used to worry about race, it's necessary to reassure the reader that the names of this recipe and the one following refer only to the color of the result, not to the source of either meat or recipe.

>6 pounds joints, bones and meat
>3 quarts water
>1 to 2 tsp. salt, or to taste
>1 tsp. whole peppercorns
>1 medium onion, chopped coarsely
>1 cup celery, chopped coarsely
>1/4 tsp. mace or sweet basil

Trim meat from bones and cube; place meat and bones in water, add 1 tsp. salt, bring to boil, and simmer covered for 2 hours, skimming frequently. Add peppercorns, onion, celery, and mace or basil; and simmer 3 hours more, still covered except when skimming. Add more salt to taste, strain through fine cheesecloth, chill, and store for later use.

BROWN STOCK

Although this is not an easy recipe to prepare, the difficulty lies only in the amount of labor involved; and the versatility of the product is more than worth the trouble involved. One cannot make too much of this staple, assuming one has sufficient storage space and immunity from over-curious missing-persons bureaus.

> 6 pounds long bones with meat; about 1/3 bone and fat, about 2/3 lean meat
> 3 quarts water
> 2 tsp. salt
> 1 tsp. whole peppercorns
> 6 whole cloves
> 1 bay leaf
> 2 tsp. thyme
> (Optional: 1/4 tsp. tarragon, 1/2 tsp. oregano)
> 1/2 cup carrots, diced
> 1/2 cup turnips, diced
> 1 small onion, chopped coarsely

Cut meat from bones, cube in 1 inch pieces. Put 2/3 of meat in kettle with fat, salt, and water; let stand 30 minutes. Crack long bones, scoop out marrow. Put bones in kettle; fry remaining 1/3 of meat with marrow in a skillet, then add to kettle. Add peppercorns and bay leaf, bring to boil, and simmer slowly, covered for 6 hours, skimming as required. Add remaining seasonings and the vegetables, cook for 90 minutes more, strain, chill, and store for later use.

STURDY SOUP

Manburger and sausage are not the only ends to which ground Man may be put:

3 pounds ground Man, lean meat
3 quarts water
1/4 pound pearl sago or cornstarch
2 cups milk
Yolks of 6 eggs
Salt and pepper

Place meat in water, bring slowly to boil, simmer 2 hours, skimming when necessary, and strain. Bring to boil again. Add sago or starch which has been soaked in just enough water to cover. Boil 30 minutes, then pour stock onto egg yolks, stirring them briskly the while. Salt and pepper to taste, serve immediately. For 6 to 12.

IMITATION ERSATZ
MOCK TURTLE SOUP

Though involved, this is a reasonably fool-proof recipe, especially well suited for some tasty but otherwise hard-to-use portions of the donor's anatomy.

1 lower leg, less calf muscle, or 1 lower arm
10 whole cloves
10 peppercorns
1/2 tsp. thyme
1 medium onion, sliced
1 pint brown stock
1 cup Madeira
1 cup stewed tomatoes

1/2 lemon
1/2 cup flour

Scrub limb, remove hair, and soak in cold water 1 hour. Put it with the cloves, peppercorns, thyme, onion, and brown stock into 1 gallon of water, bring to boil, and cook briskly until meat is tender—about 120 minutes, while skimming and reserving fat from surface. Remove limb, continue to boil water until

reduced to 3 pints, then strain. Cut meat from bone, dice. Using 3 tsp. fat that was skimmed from soup, brown the flour in deep skillet. Add brown stock, reserved soup, tomatoes, meat. Simmer 5 minutes, add juice of 1/2 lemon, Madeira, and serve at once. For 6 to 8.

BODYBUILDING STEW

Here is a simple, straightforward method of preparing a 180 pound, well muscled bodybuilder. For less ideal donors, adjust the proportions accordingly. Special requirements are a 30 gallon or larger kettle and a large, hungry horde to be fed.

> **Of 1 man, the meat in 1 to 2 inch cubes**
> **1/2 cup salt**
> **1/4 cup pepper**
> **6 quarts red wine or tomato juice**
> **1/4 cup sage or thyme**
> **5 pounds flour**

Sprinkle the cubed meat (which will amount to between 75 and 90 pounds, depending on physique) with salt and pepper, roll in flour, and brown in a large skillet or lunch-counter type grill. Mix the wine or tomato juice with 10 gallons water, bring to boil, and put in meat. Cover and simmer for 150 to 210 minutes, until tender. Serve hot, with rice or potatoes. For 150 to 200.

PERSON GUMBO

Not to be confused with the extremely spicy East African Okra Stew, Person Gumbo is a quiet soup, suitable for friends in bed with a cold, especially if they are tired of chicken soup and its legendary powers.

> 3 pounds lean Person-meat, in 3/4 by 1 by
>   1-1/2 inch pieces
> 1 small onion, chopped fine
> 3 cups cooked okra
> 1 pound fresh tomatoes, peeled and cubed
> 3 quarts white stock
> Salt and pepper to taste

Put meat in kettle with water to barely cover, cook covered for 15 minutes. Add tomatoes, cook 15 minutes more. Add okra, stock, salt and pepper to taste, bring to a boil again, and serve at once. For 8 to 12.

SCOTCH BROTH

WITH SHOULDER

Cooks, no matter how well-meaning, who persist in labeling an ordinary meat stock with a few vegetables and barley as "Scotch Broth" deserve no better than to be used for the real thing. A proper Scotch Broth is both soup and main course, all in one kettle, as explained below:

> 1 deltoid (shoulder) muscle, with bone; about 7 pounds
> 4 tsp. salt
> 1 tsp. pepper, to taste
> 1 cup barley, either pre-soaked overnight or quick-cooking
> (If desired: 1/2 cup split peas)
> 1/4 cup carrots, cubed
> 1/2 cup turnips, cubed
> 1/2 cup celery, cubed
> 1/4 cup onion, chopped coarsely
> 1 leek, sliced
> 1 tsp. fresh parsley, chopped fine

Put deltoid in a large kettle with water to cover (about 3 to 6 pints) with salt, pepper, barley, and peas if used. Bring to boil, cook briskly for 90 minutes or until tender (which, for exceptionally tough donors, may require 120 minutes). Skim off fat. Add vegetables (which may be sautéed for 5 minutes in the skimmed fat before adding, if desired). Cook for about 30 minutes, until vegetables are done. Remove meat to a hot, covered platter; serve soup, sprinkled with parsley; then serve meat, sliced, with potatoes and cabbage. For 8 to 12.

IRISH STEW

This is plain, hearty fare. A reasonable variation is permissible, but potatoes are an absolute must. Getting the donor "stewed" before dispatching him doesn't help the taste; but then again, it doesn't seem to hurt either.

> 3 pounds Man, in 1 to 1-1/2 inch cubes
> 1 medium onion, sliced
> 1/2 cup carrots, cubed
> 1/2 cup turnips, cubed
> 1 pound potato, cubed
> 1 pound potato, in very thin slices
> 3 tsp. salt, to taste
> 1/2 tsp. pepper, to taste
> Chopped parsley

Bring 3 pints water to a boil, add meat. Boil (always covered) 60 minutes. Add carrots, turnips, cubed potato, boil 30 minutes more. Add sliced potato, simmer 30 minutes more. Add salt, pepper, sprinkle with parsley, and serve hot. For 6.

PHILADELPHIA PEPPER POT

PERSON SOUP

The "Pepper" in the name is traditional, rather than denoting a highly seasoned dish. While some authorities assert that the reticulum of a ruminant makes a better soup than the one stomach of Man, one must make do with what comes to hand.

    1 stomach, in 1/2 inch pieces
    1 medium onion, chopped
    1 stalk celery, chopped
    1 green pepper, chopped
    1/2 pound potato, cubed
    3-4 tbsp. flour
    1 quart white stock
    (1/2 cup heavy cream, optional)
    2 tsp. salt, to taste
    1/2 tsp. pepper or more, to taste
    Cooking oil

Sauté vegetables 15 minutes. Add flour, sauté 5 minutes more. Add meat and white stock, cover, and simmer 1 hour. (Stir in heavy cream, if used.) Serve hot. For 6.

BASQUE BLOOD SOUP

Interestingly enough, this recipe is unknown in Transylvania.

    Fresh blood
    Salt
    Pepper
    Cayenne
    Grated onion

Pour blood in bowl, season *heavily* with salt, pepper, and cayenne. Garnish with grated onion, and serve.

MULLIGATAWNY OF MAN

Literally, "pepper-water," this is a kind of curry-soup from India. As in all such spicy dishes, season cautiously.

    1/2 pound lean Man, diced
    1-1/2 quarts white stock
    1 pound fresh tomatoes, peeled and diced
    1/4 cup celery, chopped
    1 medium carrot, chopped fine
    2 sweet red peppers, chopped
    1 apple, diced
    1/4 cup flour
    1/2 to 2 tsp. curry powder, to taste
    1/2 tsp. ground cloves
    1 tsp. salt, or to taste
    1 tsp. pepper, or to taste

Brown meat in heavy skillet. Add vegetables, stock, flour, and spices; simmer covered for 1 hour. Strain, reserving stock. Return meat to stock. Purée vegetables from strainer in a sieve or blender, return to stock. Season resulting soup with salt and pepper to taste. Serves 6. (The "normal" seasoning of curry powder is 1 tsp., but both tastes and curry vary widely. Remember, it is easier to add curry later, than to take out too much!)

WEST AFRICAN

PEANUT & PERSON SOUP

This dish must really be approached with caution; some people may be allergic to peanuts (called "groundnuts" by Great Britons) and others may find the cayenne pretty overwhelming. Except as a matter of courtesy, it is not necessary to inquire into the allergies of the donor, however.

    1 pound of person, in 1-1/2 inch cubes
    2 tbsp. flour
    1 large eggplant, chopped
    1 can tomatoes
    2 cups peanuts, shelled and roasted
    3 cloves garlic, chopped
    1 tsp. salt, to taste
    1 tsp. cayenne, to taste
    1 tsp. cooking oil

In a heavy skillet, brown meat, adding garlic as it browns. Add 2 quarts water, bring to a boil, and simmer covered for 40 minutes. In a second skillet, heat peanuts, crushing with a potato masher as they get hot. Add warmed peanuts to soup, add eggplant, tomatoes, salt, and cayenne. Simmer 20 minutes more, and serve with a medium fire extinguisher. For 6 to 8.

EAST AFRICAN OKRA STEW

Although not as ferociously spiced as Peanut & Person Soup or Curry, this is still a dish that must be eaten with some caution and large water glasses.

    3 pounds of lean Man, in 1 to 2 inch cubes
    2 large onions, chopped fine
    1 pound of fresh okra, cut up
    4 cloves garlic

> 4 to 6 oz. tomato paste
> 2 tsp. salt, or to taste
> 1 tsp. pepper, or to taste

Brown meat and onion in a large skillet. Crush garlic in a press and add. Mix tomato paste with 3 cups of water in a mixing bowl; when well mixed, add to meat. Simmer, covered, 40 minutes. Salt and pepper to taste, and serve hot. For 6 to 8.

ARABIAN
TOMATO & INFIDEL SOUP

Our source didn't make it clear whether "Infidel" refers to the violation of the Mohammedan dietary laws involved in eating the stuff, or to the kind of person who should be used for this recipe. Whatever the religious practices of the donor, however, the tougher cuts such as calf or thigh are best suited as ingredients here.

> 3 pounds of Man, in one piece
> 3 large tomatoes, cut in 8 pieces each
> 3 small onions, chopped fine
> 6 leaves of mint, cut fine (do *not* use liquid essence of mint)
> 2 oz. of rice
> 2 tsp. salt, to taste
> 1 tsp. pepper, to taste

In a deep skillet, brown meat, then onion. The meat should self-oil, but an especially lean Person may require a tsp. of cooking oil to start him properly. Add 2 quarts water, tomatoes, mint. Bring to boil and simmer, covered, for 90 minutes. Remove meat, put rice into soup. Cut meat into small pieces, about 1 inch cubes, and return to soup. Simmer 10 minutes more. Serves 6 to 8.

HUNTER STEW

Although Hungarians are not essential for making Hungarian Goulash, nor members of other ethnos to recipes for their ethnic dishes, this recipe is intended specifically for the disposal of stray hunters, whether shot accidentally by their colleagues or on purpose by irate farmers. While the recipe specifies specific kinds of meat, substitutions may be made freely.

> **5 pounds cubed Man**
> **3-1/2 pounds Venison, sliced thin**
> **1 pound cubed Dog**
> **1/4 pound butter**
> **3 carrots, diced**
> **2 small turnips, diced**
> **2 medium onions, diced**
> **1 large stalk celery, diced**
> **1 large *bouquet garni***
> **1 cup dry sherry**
> **Salt and pepper to taste**

Melt butter in a large iron kettle. Add meat and onions, brown well. Add water to barely cover. Salt and pepper heavily. Simmer gently for 90 minutes, adding water as needed. Skim off grease, add diced vegetables, simmer gently for 30 to 45 minutes more. Stir in the sherry and serve at once. For 20.

INDEX